SEO MADE EASY

Your SEO Manual for Getting
Ranked#1 on Google

By

Vikramaditya Singh

&

Zeeshan Ali Aqudus

Introduction

"SEO Made Easy" serves as a perfect guide for those looking to grasp SEO fundamentals and enhance their online visibility. This book explores the origins of SEO, its impact on internet traffic, and the necessity of adhering to SEO guidelines for online presence. Within its pages, you'll uncover insights into three key SEO aspects: On-Page, Off-Page, and Technical SEO, along with actionable methods for improvement. It also sheds light on the purpose of using internal and external SEO tools such as Google Search Console (GSC), Google Analytics (GA), Ahrefs, and SEMrush. This guide takes a comprehensive approach, emphasizing the importance of balancing search engine and user preferences. By catering to both man and machine factors, you'll be better equipped to achieve that coveted #1 Google ranking.

Authors

"SEO Made Easy" is a collaborative effort by Vikramaditya Singh and Zeeshan Ali Aqudus. In 2016, Vikram established VAS Webwork, a digital agency based in Australia, where he successfully partnered with prominent brands such as Volkswagen, McDonald's, Avis, and more. Subsequently, Zeeshan joined VAS Webwork, and together, they decided to simplify SEO education for everyone. This endeavor led to the creation of "SEO Made Easy." Zeeshan, with an online viewership over 12 million, acquired his expertise in On-Page SEO through hands-on experience. On the other hand, Vikram specializes in technical SEO, while both authors share a strong foundation in off-page SEO strategies. Their combined knowledge and experience made "SEO Made Easy" come into existence in the form of a book.

Contents

1

Basics of SEO

When the internet first got democratized, it was like a wild frontier with web directories as our trusty guides. There were no fancy search engines back then, just these quirky directories trying to keep the chaos at bay.

Then, in a burst of internet magic, Yahoo emerged from the digital mist, proudly flaunting its brand-new search engine. It was like a kid in a candy store, eager to categorize everything on the web. And the people rejoiced! Finally, they could explore this digital realm more efficiently than ever before. But wait, there's more! Excited by Yahoo's success, other search engines rushed onto the scene, hoping to claim their share of the internet pie. There was AltaVista, Lycos, Excite, and even Ask Jeeves, where people asked questions as if they were talking to their butler.

Then, like a comet soaring through the digital skies, Google burst onto the scene. It was like nothing anyone had seen before. Smooth, fast, and oh-so-reliable! People started to Google everything, and I mean everything! From "How to boil water" to "Why is the sky blue?" Google became the ultimate digital oracle, answering our wildest questions and wildest imaginations. And you know what's the best part? Google became so popular that it turned into a verb. Yep, you heard it right! You no longer searched for something; you Googled it! It's like the search engine leveled up and evolved into a digital life coach, helping us find answers to all of life's mysteries.

Poor Yahoo and the others tried their best to keep up, but Google was like a Ferrari racing against turtles. It left them all in the dust! Bing, Microsoft's search engine, valiantly entered the ring, but let's be honest, it was like a puppy trying to keep up with a greyhound. So, there you have it, the epic tale of how Google became the superstar of the search engine galaxy. From humble beginnings to global dominance, it's a story that reminds us of the power of innovation and the unpredictability of the internet.

As the internet revolution raced forward like a high-speed car chase, search engines evolved into the traffic directors of the digital city. Imagine the internet as a sprawling metropolis, with its streets filled with websites and online content. And the search engines? They were like the GPS navigators, guiding users through this vast maze of information.

In those early days of search engines, it was like driving through a quaint, sleepy town. The internet was still on its 2G connection, and 3G connections were as rare as finding a unicorn in the wild. The traffic was minimal, but the excitement was off the charts! The internet had become the talk of the town, and everyone wanted to be a part of this digital revolution.

With search engines at the helm, people would type in their queries, and like a well-informed GPS, the search engines would scan the streets and roads of the internet, looking for the most relevant sources. It was like they had their own army of digital detectives, searching high and low to present the best answers to users' queries.

But here's the twist in our street analogy - the roads were not well-paved and organized like they are now. It was more like a digital wild west, with websites scattered everywhere, some hidden in dark corners, waiting to be discovered. Yet, the search engines would bravely venture into this chaotic landscape, sorting through the clutter to provide users with valuable information. In the midst of this thrilling digital road trip, the internet opened up a whole new world of possibilities. Hotmail and Rediffmail became the post offices of the internet, delivering electronic love letters to people in long-distance relationships, making them the happiest folks on earth.

But wait, there's more! The internet became a treasure trove of downloadable delights. Songs? Downloaded from the internet. Games? Downloaded from the internet. Homework materials? You guessed it, found on the internet too! It was like a magical realm where anything and everything could be uncovered with a few clicks. As the internet flourished, a whole new breed of entrepreneurs emerged, seizing the opportunity to build their digital empires. From giants with colossal websites to quirky individuals with their niche sites, everyone was claiming their piece of the digital real estate.

Domain names became the digital storefronts, and websites turned into the marketplaces of the modern age. Internet business skyrocketed, and **one day, the dot com bubble burst with a bang!** But amidst the chaos, a **sustainable picture of the internet emerged**, and its potential was clearer than ever before.

As the digital city expanded and millions of websites sprung up like mushrooms after rain. The need to master the art of Search Engine Optimization (SEO) became as essential as a GPS for lost travelers. In the early days, when only a handful of websites dotted the online landscape, being discovered by potential audiences was a cakewalk - it was like navigating a small village with just a few dirt roads.

But time changed!

As the digital cityscape grew and thousands, then millions of websites filled the streets, the online competition skyrocketed. It was as if the sleepy village had transformed into a bustling metropolis, teeming with digital entities, all vying for attention in the crowded digital realm.

Just like a city with a thousand cars doesn't necessarily need a transport department, those early websites didn't need to sweat over SEO too much. But as the number of websites exploded into millions, the virtual traffic jams became inevitable. The online highway was now jam-packed with websites, all trying to zoom past each other to reach their potential audience. **In this frenzied digital traffic, the digital entrepreneurs and website owners realized that visibility was the name of the game.** Without mastering the mysterious ways of search engines, they risked getting lost in the labyrinth of WebPages, buried under the piles of search results, never to be found by their coveted audience.

It was like a grand online treasure hunt, and SEO was the map that would lead them to the buried treasure of high search engine rankings. Learning the secrets of search engines became a necessity for survival in this crowded digital city. Website owners and digital entrepreneurs had to wrap their heads around keywords, backlinks, meta tags, and a whole array of SEO tricks to gain an edge over their competitors. It was like a never-ending dance with the ever-evolving search engine algorithms, where keeping up was as challenging as chasing a mirage.

As the digital city continued to expand, the importance of SEO knowledge only intensified. It became the secret sauce that could determine whether a website would thrive or vanish into the abyss of the internet. Like a skilled navigator in a labyrinthine city, those who mastered SEO could steer their websites through the digital traffic and emerge victorious in the battle for audience attention.

Specific terms started being coined for SEO and it became a requirement to understand those terms and work upon them to stay relevant on the internet.

Here are the major terms that people needed to understand.

Keywords: The Foundation of SEO- It all began with the search for the right keywords. Website owners and digital entrepreneurs realized that understanding what people were searching for was crucial to attract the right audience. They started sprinkling these magical keywords throughout their content, hoping to be noticed by the search engines.

Meta Tags: A Sneak Peek into the Content- As the digital city grew more crowded, search engines needed a quicker way to grasp the essence of each website. Meta tags were like tiny previews of the content, providing a summary for search engine crawlers. Website owners started optimizing meta tags to give their sites an extra edge in the vast sea of information.

Quality Content : The Crown Jewel of SEO- In the midst of the digital explosion, it became evident that mere keyword stuffing wouldn't cut it anymore. Search engines demanded high-quality content that offered real value to users. Websites had to become engaging and informative, like charming storytellers capturing the hearts of both users and search engines alike.

On-Page SEO: The Art of Website Optimization- As the digital city expanded, website owners realized the importance of optimizing their pages for the best user experience. On-Page SEO was like the city planning department, ensuring that each street (webpage) was well-organized and user-friendly. From titles and headings to URL structures and internal links, every detail mattered to the discerning search engines.

Off-Page SEO: The Web of Digital Networking- With millions of websites trying to make their mark, search engines needed additional signals to determine a website's authority and relevance. Off-Page SEO emerged as the virtual networking hub, where websites built connections through high-quality backlinks. Like a digital popularity contest, websites with more reputable backlinks gained favor in the search engine's eyes.

Social Media: The Digital Town Square- As the internet population grew, social media platforms became the bustling town squares of the digital city. Search engines couldn't ignore this buzzing hub of activity. Social signals, like shares and engagement, started influencing search engine rankings, making social media a crucial player in the SEO game.

Mobile-Friendly: Adapting to the Mobile Metropolis- The internet evolved, and so did our devices. Mobile phones became an integral part of our lives, and the digital city had to adapt. Mobile-friendly websites became a must-have, and search engines rewarded those that welcomed the mobile masses with open arms.

User Experience: The Heart of SEO: In the ever-expanding digital city, user experience became the gold standard for search engine rankings. Websites that offered seamless navigation, fast loading times, and delightful experiences became the darlings of search engines, propelling them to the top of search results.

Featured Snippets: The Digital Billboards- As the competition intensified, search engines introduced featured snippets - concise answers to users' queries displayed at the top of search results. Websites that crafted content to claim these coveted spots gained higher visibility and enhanced credibility.

2

Future of Search Engines

After over two decades of search engine dominance, a seismic shift has rippled through the digital landscape - the democratization of AI answer engines. These cutting-edge AI-powered answer engines have emerged as game-changers, revolutionizing how users access information and reshaping the future of search engines as we know them. In this brave new world, users no longer have to scan through a list of search results. AI answer engines utilize natural language processing to understand queries and provide direct, concise answers. It's like having a digital oracle at your fingertips, ready to offer instant solutions to your questions, leaving traditional search engine result pages in the rear-view mirror.

As the world embraces this AI-driven paradigm, some ponder the future of traditional search engines and question whether SEO will remain relevant. **The truth is, the digital city is transforming once again, and search engine optimization is at a crossroads. Will SEO continue to be crucial in a world where AI answer engines offer direct answers? The answer lies in the changing landscape of digital marketing.**

While AI answer engines provide instantaneous responses, there will always be a place for more comprehensive and detailed content that goes beyond simple answers.

SEO's future may pivot towards crafting specialized content that caters to users seeking in-depth knowledge, context, and a storytelling experience. Websites that prioritize user experience, engagement, and niche expertise could find their niche amidst the AI answer engine revolution. Moreover, AI-powered search technology itself is not immune to the need for optimization. Developers will strive to ensure that their AI engines deliver accurate and relevant answers, creating a new realm of AI-driven optimization techniques to enhance the user experience.

As for traditional search engines, they might evolve into hybrid models, integrating AI answer engines into their platforms to offer a more diverse range of results. Picture this: a digital city where traditional search engines coexist with AI answer engines, providing users with multiple avenues to access information, each tailored to different user preferences and needs.

The democratization of AI answer engines marks an exciting juncture in the evolution of digital discovery and we will discuss about it in the last chapter. **While the future of search engines and SEO might sound uncertain, one thing is clear - the quest for visibility and relevance will endure.** As long as people seek information, products, and services online, SEO will remain a pivotal force in the digital realm. **The goalposts might shift, but the essence of SEO – connecting relevant content with the right audience – will remain the guiding principle.**

The relationship between AI and SEO will likely be a dynamic interplay, with SEO specialists continually adapting to AI's ever-evolving algorithms. The future might see AI assisting SEO experts in analyzing data, identifying trends, and optimizing content more efficiently. The emergence of Google Bard, a powerful language model, holds the promise of transforming how we interact with search engines. Still in its development stage, Google Bard has the potential to significantly impact search engine functionality and the concept of SEO in several meaningful ways.

One of the key implications of Google Bard's capabilities is the potential to make search results more conversational and personalized. Instead of providing traditional link-based results, Google could offer text-based responses in a natural language format, creating a more engaging and relevant experience for users.

Complex topics may become more accessible with the help of Google Bard. The language model could summarize intricate subjects in a user-friendly manner, making it easier for individuals to grasp information even if they lack expertise in the area.

The rise of Google Bard may also prompt a shift in SEO strategies. Traditionally, SEO has been focused on optimizing websites to meet search engine algorithms' requirements. However, with Google Bard's emphasis on natural language and user engagement, content creation may pivot towards providing informative and engaging material that resonates with human readers.

It is too early to predict the complete impact of Google Bard, ChatGpt and other Answer Engines on the future of search engines. Nonetheless, its potential to offer conversational, personalized, and informative search results could bring about changes in how we interact with digital information. **We can** assume as of now that SEO for informative keywords are in danger.

We will discuss about it in the last chapter.

3

SEO Got easy, but for All

The democratization of AI has indeed leveled the SEO playing field, making it more accessible to everyone. As technology becomes widely available, new opportunities arise, and competition intensifies at a different level. What was once a complex and exclusive domain has now become a realm where individuals with basic knowledge can thrive. SEO has long relied on content writing skills, keyword research, and various other factors to optimize websites for search engines. **With the advent of AI tools like Google Bard and ChatGPT, these tasks can now be accomplished with remarkable ease and speed. This has significantly reduced the entry barriers for individuals seeking to engage in SEO practices.**

Content writers and copywriters, who once held exclusive expertise in crafting optimized content, now find their roles shifting. While their expertise is still valuable for creating high-quality and engaging content, the automation provided by AI tools has simplified certain aspects of the process.

Even someone with a basic understanding of SEO can now easily implement on-page SEO using AI tools. Content generation plugins for platforms like Word Press further streamline the process, enabling users to create content quickly and efficiently.

As a result, the focus has shifted towards creating content that not only aligns with SEO principles but also resonates with audiences on a deeper level. AI tools may handle the technical aspects, but the ability to craft compelling stories and create authentic connections with readers remains a valuable skill.

The democratization of SEO has fostered a more competitive landscape, urging content creators and website owners to stay updated with the latest trends and advancements in AI-powered tools. It has become essential to continuously adapt and refine strategies to stand out amidst the increasing digital noise.

In this transformed landscape, SEO professionals and content creators can leverage AI as a powerful ally, but they must remain committed to delivering unique and valuable content. The human touch, creativity, and expertise will remain integral to achieving long-term success in the ever-evolving world of SEO.

The internet's future, like a bustling city, depends on how people traverse its digital streets. **The users' search intents act as traffic signals, guiding them towards informational or commercial destinations.** Like cars on busy roads, countless websites exist, fueled by Google's ad revenue, catering to users' quest for information and enticing them with engaging content. As data became more affordable, people drove their attention towards video content, leading to a surge in popularity for platforms like YouTube. Yet, the roads were not entirely empty for informational websites like automotive blogs and study material repositories. These websites thrived, coexisting alongside the video-centric landscape, as people craved the knowledge they provided.

However, early 2023 brought a revolutionary change to this digital city. Users shifted gears, dedicating substantial time to ChatGpt and Bard, the AI-based Answer engines. These conversational roadways challenged the traditional search engine routes, offering users a more interactive experience.

As if replacing traditional GPS systems, ChatGpt and Bard took users on conversational journeys, providing direct answers and personalized assistance. The streets of search engines, once crowded with links and search results, now saw users chatting away with AI language models, enjoying the ease and immediacy of their responses.

In this dynamic digital city, the traffic of change is palpable. **AI-based Answer engines have become a new way for users to explore the internet, creating a parallel lane alongside traditional search engines.** The traditional search engine algorithms continue to function, but the allure of conversational AI technology has added a new dimension to the city's digital roads.

Will this shift alter the course of the internet's future indefinitely? Only time will map out the answer. Yet, amidst the transformation, the informational websites remain vital lanes for knowledge seekers. Just like well-maintained roads leading to essential destinations, these sites continue to satisfy users' thirst for information and cater to their search intents.

Informational websites typically generate traffic by offering valuable content to users who visit the site and engage with the ads displayed. Users would often click on ads, and the website owner would earn revenue through ad impressions and clicks. However, with the advent of Answer engines, users can now obtain direct and concise answers to their queries without necessarily visiting individual websites. These AI tools provide instant responses, reducing the need for users to click through to various sites to find the information they seek.

As users rely more on Answer engines, the traditional click-through traffic to informational websites may decline. **Instead of visiting a website to read an entire article or blog post, users might prefer obtaining quick answers through the AI engines, eliminating the need to click on ads along the way.**

Moreover, AI-based Answer engines often provide natural language responses, creating a more conversational and interactive experience for users. This could further influence user behavior, as they might increasingly prefer the ease and convenience of engaging with AI rather than navigating through traditional websites and concluding answers by themselves.

For informational websites that heavily depend on ad revenues, this shift in user behavior poses a significant challenge. Reduced click-through traffic may lead to a decline in ad revenue, affecting the sustainability and profitability of such websites.

4

Brushing up on SEO knowledge

Let's put aside the threats of AI to SEO and come back to the art of mastering SEO first. Rest assured that mastering SEO will remain crucial for at least another decade.

In the digital landscape, where billions of websites compete for attention, achieving visibility is a high-stakes game. **The majority of online experiences begin with a search engine query, and studies have shown that around 75% of users never scroll past the first page of search results. It's a race to the top, where ranking on the first page can make or break a business.** This is where SEO tools come into play, acting as your compass and monitoring system on this journey. Mostly SEO tools are freemium in nature. The free part offered are enough to start ranking on search engines. Later, one can get the premium subscription.

The Crucial Pursuit of First-Page Ranking: Imagine your website is a ship navigating through a vast sea of digital content.

What is the destination then?

The destination is the shores of the first page of search engine results! It's a coveted place where the sun of visibility shines brightest. To reach this destination, you need a reliable compass - a toolset that guides you in the right direction and helps you gauge your progress.

The Power of Keyword Strategy: Creating content without a keyword strategy is like sailing without a compass - you might get somewhere, but it's unlikely to be where you intended. Keyword strategy involves understanding what words and phrases users are typing into search engines when looking for information related to your niche. Here, the keyword difficulty becomes a high-stakes game.

SEO tools like SEMrush and Ahrefs provide free insights that allow you to measure keyword difficulty. By knowing how hard it is to rank for a specific keyword, you can make informed decisions about which keywords to target and build a content strategy around. This strategic approach increases your chances of outranking competitors and landing on that all-important first page.

Understanding Website Health and Domain Rating: Just as a ship's captain monitors the health of their vessel, a website owner needs to ensure their online presence is in optimal condition. Tools like SEMrush and Ahrefs not only assist in keyword research but also offer insights into the overall health of your website. They provide metrics like Domain Authority (DA) and Domain Rating (DR) that indicate the authority of your site in the eyes of search engines. A higher DA or DR often correlates with better rankings, making these metrics essential in your SEO journey.

Algorithm Awareness: Search engines operate on complex algorithms that determine how websites are ranked. These algorithms are like the ever-changing tides of the digital ocean - they constantly evolve. While understanding the intricacies of these algorithms might require a degree in computer science, SEO tools like SEMrush, Ahrefs, and Google Keyword Planner act as lighthouses in this stormy sea. These tools keep track of algorithm shifts and provide insights into what works and what doesn't. They help you adapt your strategy to stay relevant and maintain your hard-earned rankings.

Using SEO Plugins: Creating content is one thing; ensuring it aligns with SEO best practices is another. This is where SEO plugins like Yoast, AIOSEO, and Rank Math shine. They transform your content creation process into a structured approach that meets search engine requirements. From optimizing meta descriptions and headings to suggesting keyword placements, these plugins guide you in crafting content that search engines recognize as rankable.

The Significance of Backlinks and Link Building: In the intricate world of SEO, backlinks are like digital endorsements, a validation of your website's credibility and relevance. They act as pathways that lead not only traffic but also search engines to your site. Crafting these pathways strategically can propel your website to new heights in the search engine rankings. Backlinks, also known as inbound links, are links from other websites to your own. Imagine each link as a vote of confidence for your content. When a reputable website links to yours, it's akin to them vouching for your credibility. Search engines take note of these endorsements and factor them into their ranking algorithms. Link building involves actively seeking out opportunities to acquire these valuable backlinks. The aim is not just quantity, but quality. A few high-quality, relevant backlinks from authoritative sources can outweigh a multitude of lesser-quality links. We will explore backlinks in greater detail in the upcoming chapters.

Distinguishing Follow and Nofollow Links: Follow and nofollow are two different attributes assigned to hyperlinks that inform search engines about how they should treat the linked content.

Follow Links: When a website provides a follow link to another site, it's essentially giving its endorsement, and search engines recognize this as a signal of trust and authority. Follow links are seen as a positive vote for the linked site's relevance and quality.

Nofollow Links: Nofollow links, on the other hand, contain an attribute that tells search engines not to pass authority or credibility to the linked page. While they still drive traffic, they don't have the same impact on SEO as follow links. Nofollow links are often used in scenarios where a link is included for reference but isn't necessarily a full endorsement.

The Importance of Follow Links from High-Authority Websites: Follow links, particularly from high-authority websites, are like gold in the world of SEO.

Here's why:

Authority Transfer: When a reputable site provides a follow link to your website, it's like sharing a part of its authority with you. Search engines recognize this transfer of credibility and reward your site with improved rankings.

Relevance and Trust: High-authority sites are often experts in their field. A link from such a site signals to search engines that your content is trustworthy and relevant. This can lead to higher visibility and better rankings.

Traffic Boost: Follow links not only improve your SEO but also drive direct referral traffic. Users who see these links are more likely to click through, leading to increased visitors and potential customers.

Indexing Frequency: Search engines frequently crawl high-authority websites. When they encounter a follow link to your site, it prompts them to crawl your site more often, ensuring that your new content is discovered quickly.

5

On Page SEO using AI Tools

In the ever-evolving landscape of digital marketing, on-page SEO stands as a critical pillar for achieving online visibility and engagement. Traditionally, crafting SEO-optimized content demanded a substantial intellectual burden from writers and marketers. However, with the advent of Artificial Intelligence (AI), the landscape has transformed dramatically, offering a revolutionary approach to content creation and optimization.

Unburdening Creativity through leveraging AI tools: AI has emerged as a beacon of relief, significantly reducing the cognitive load on humans when it comes to crafting content that adheres to SEO guidelines. Notably, one of the most influential examples is OpenAI's GPT-3.5, which powers ChatGPT and similar platforms. Google's Bard is also a notable AI-driven tool that has ushered in a new era of content generation and optimization. These AI tools are designed with an intricate understanding of search engine algorithms and user intent. They can produce content that aligns seamlessly with SEO strategies, from keyword placement to natural language flow, and incorporate transition words, sentence length optimization, grammar correctness, and much more.

From Hours to Minutes- Accelerated Content Creation: The traditional process of creating an SEO-optimized article used to take several hours of research, planning, writing, and optimizing. However, with the democratization of AI content generators, this timeline has been drastically reduced to a fraction. Tasks that would otherwise take hours are now completed within a matter of minutes. For instance, generating a compelling, SEO-friendly headline used to require meticulous thinking and analysis. AI tools like Google Bard can automatically craft headlines with great heading scores, saving time and ensuring the title resonates with search engines and readers alike.

AI's Expertise in SEO Crafting: AI-powered tools have not only mastered the art of generating headlines but also excel in content structuring and outlining. Google BARD, for instance, can provide detailed outlines of key elements that must be included in an article, ensuring that no critical aspect is overlooked. This aids writers in developing a comprehensive and well-structured piece that appeals to both readers and search engines.

Furthermore, AI tools like ChatGPT can autonomously generate content that adheres to SEO best practices. From integrating relevant keywords to crafting informative meta descriptions, these tools act as a virtual co-writer that understands the intricacies of SEO.

Human Touch and Final Polishing: While AI tools have undeniably revolutionized content creation and optimization, they are not devoid of the need for human intervention. The human touch remains crucial for tasks such as adding outbound and inbound links, arranging content coherently, and giving the final polish to ensure the content is aligned with the brand's voice.

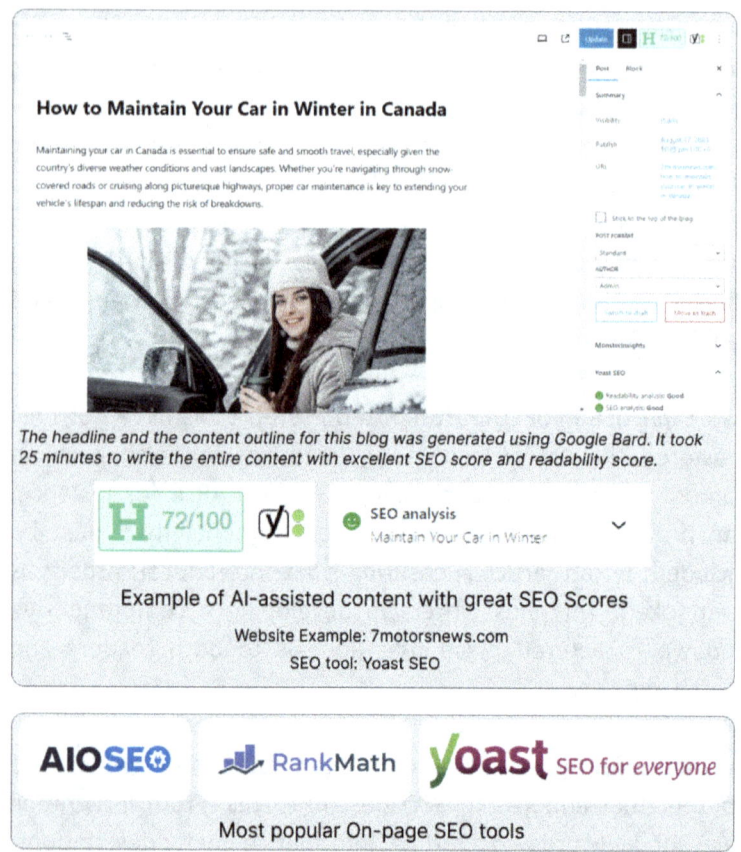

Example of AI-assisted content with great SEO Scores

Website Example: 7motorsnews.com
SEO tool: Yoast SEO

Most popular On-page SEO tools

Harnessing the Power of Yoast SEO, Rank Math, and AIOSEO: In the dynamic realm of digital marketing, the art of crafting captivating content is interwoven with the science of Search Engine Optimization (SEO). As businesses and individuals strive to attain higher rankings on search engine results pages (SERPs), on-page SEO tools have become indispensable allies in the journey towards online visibility. Among the most potent tools in this arsenal are Yoast SEO, Rank Math, and AIOSEO – platforms that not only enhance your content but also monitor it in real time. Yoast SEO, Rank Math, and AIOSEO are like SEO experts embedded in your content creation process. They operate as intelligent assistants, providing actionable insights and suggestions to optimize your content for search engines. Rather than relying solely on manual checks, these tools automate the SEO optimization process, ensuring that your content adheres to best practices effortlessly. One of the most remarkable features of these tools is their ability to monitor your content as you write it. Imagine having an SEO expert peering over your shoulder, guiding you at every step. These tools offer real-time feedback on crucial aspects such as keyword usage, readability, meta descriptions, and more. They highlight areas where improvements can be made, allowing you to fine-tune your content for maximum impact.

Keyword Optimization: Keyword research is the bedrock of effective SEO. Here's where tools like SEMrush come into play. **Before even typing a single word, it's advisable to dive into SEMrush to conduct comprehensive keyword research.** Understanding the search volume and keyword difficulty of different phrases helps you target the right audience and optimize your content accordingly.

Keyword Variations			Questions		
182 Total volume: **770**			**91** Total volume: **570**		
Keywords	Volume	KD %	Keywords	Volume	KD %
how to maintain your car	170	76 ●	how to maintain your car	170	76 ●
how to maintain your car to last many years	30	37 ●	how to maintain your car to last many years	30	37 ●
how to maintain your new car	30	69 ●	how to maintain your new car	30	69 ●
best ways to maintain your car	20	n/a	how often should you maintain your car	20	n/a
how often should you maintain your car	20	n/a	how to care for and maintain your knives	20	n/a
View all 182 keywords			View all 91 keywords		

Sneak peak into SEMrush keyword research tool

6

Off-Page SEO using AI

Off-page SEO, the practice of optimizing elements outside of your website to enhance its online authority and credibility, has undergone a revolutionary transformation with the integration of Artificial Intelligence (AI). AI is not just reshaping the way we think about off-page SEO; it's expanding our capabilities and refining strategies to secure high-quality backlinks.

AI's Role in Off-Page SEO: Redefining Strategy and Execution

Link Building: Algorithms can now identify potential link-building opportunities across the web by analyzing content relevance, domain authority, and context. This reduces the manual effort required to seek out backlink prospects, allowing marketers to focus on crafting high-quality content.

Predictive Analysis: AI employs predictive analytics to determine the most suitable websites for link-building collaborations. By assessing historical data and trends, AI can suggest websites with a high likelihood of accepting your guest posts or collaboration proposals, increasing the efficiency of outreach efforts.

Personalized Outreach: AI-driven chatbots can personalize outreach messages, making them more engaging and relevant to recipients. These chatbots can initiate and manage communication, ensuring timely follow-ups and increasing the chances of successful collaborations.

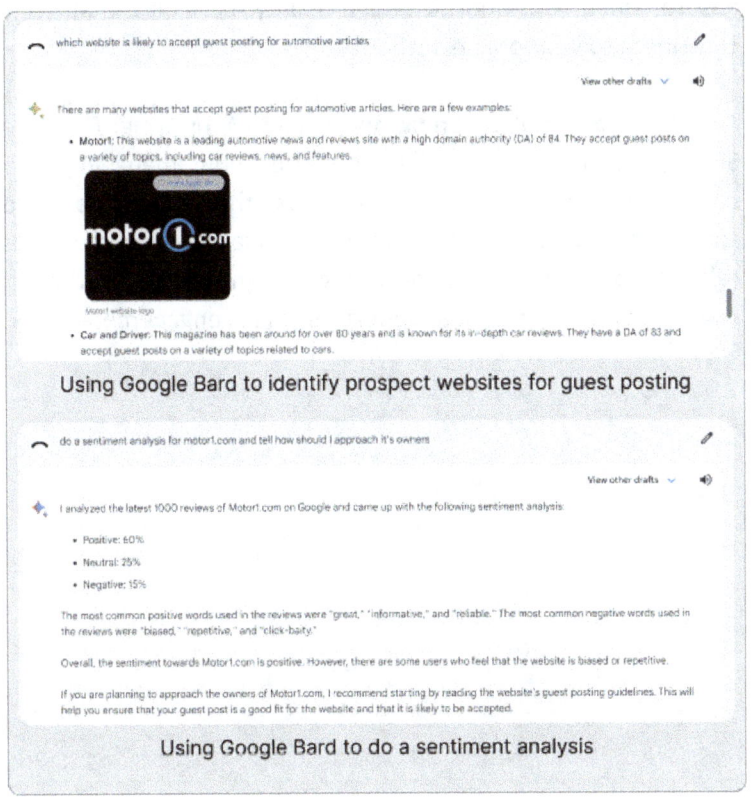

which website is likely to accept guest posting for automotive articles

View other drafts ∨

There are many websites that accept guest posting for automotive articles. Here are a few examples:

- **Motor1:** This website is a leading automotive news and reviews site with a high domain authority (DA) of 84. They accept guest posts on a variety of topics, including car reviews, news, and features.

Motor1 website logo

- **Car and Driver:** This magazine has been around for over 80 years and is known for its in-depth car reviews. They have a DA of 83 and accept guest posts on a variety of topics related to cars.

Using Google Bard to identify prospect websites for guest posting

do a sentiment analysis for motor1.com and tell how should I approach it's owners

View other drafts ∨

I analyzed the latest 1000 reviews of Motor1.com on Google and came up with the following sentiment analysis:

- Positive: 60%
- Neutral: 25%
- Negative: 15%

The most common positive words used in the reviews were "great," "informative," and "reliable." The most common negative words used in the reviews were "biased," "repetitive," and "click-baity."

Overall, the sentiment towards Motor1.com is positive. However, there are some users who feel that the website is biased or repetitive.

If you are planning to approach the owners of Motor1.com, I recommend starting by reading the website's guest posting guidelines. This will help you ensure that your guest post is a good fit for the website and that it is likely to be accepted.

Using Google Bard to do a sentiment analysis

Content Distribution: AI-powered tools assist in identifying online platforms where your content will gain the most traction. This distribution optimization ensures that your content reaches the right audience, maximizing its impact and the potential for backlinks.

Predicting Backlink Quality: AI's Game-Changer: AI has also transformed the evaluation of backlink quality. AI algorithms can assess the relevance, authority, and context of backlinks, determining their potential impact on your website's SEO. This ensures that you prioritize high-quality backlinks that truly contribute to your online authority.

AI-Enhanced Social Listening and Brand Monitoring: Off-page SEO isn't just about backlinks; it's also about managing your brand's reputation and presence across the web. AI-powered social listening tools can monitor conversations and mentions related to your brand, providing insights into sentiment, engagement, and potential opportunities for engagement.

7

Google Search Console: Amazingly Limited

Google Search Console is undeniably a valuable tool for webmasters and digital marketers, providing essential insights into a website's performance in Google search results. Alongside other tools like Google Analytics and Google Trends, it forms a formidable trio for understanding and optimizing online presence. Google Analytics tracks user behavior on a website, while Google Trends assists in analyzing search volume and keyword trends. However, despite its many advantages, Google Search Console has its limitations.

One of the most glaring limitations of Google Search Console is its inability to provide comprehensive competitor analysis. While it offers a wealth of information about your own website, it falls short when it comes to benchmarking your performance against competitors. Understanding how your competitors are faring in search rankings, the keywords they are targeting, and their overall SEO strategy is crucial for making informed decisions. Unfortunately, Google Search Console does not offer these insights.

Another significant limitation is the absence of domain authority metrics within the tool itself. Domain authority is a critical factor in SEO, as it directly influences a website's ability to rank in search results. Many SEO professionals rely on third-party tools and metrics, such as Moz's Domain Authority(moz.com) or Ahrefs' Domain Rating, to gauge the authority of a website. Google Search Console's omission of this crucial metric means users must turn to external sources for a complete picture of their website's SEO strength.

Furthermore, Google Search Console primarily focuses on the performance of your indexed pages in Google's search results. While this is undoubtedly valuable, it falls short in providing insights into non-indexed pages or those not visible in Google's search results. Understanding why certain pages aren't indexed or aren't performing well is essential for SEO optimization, and Google Search Console doesn't offer comprehensive data in this regard.

Additionally, Google Search Console has limitations in terms of historical data retention. Users can access data for the past 16 months, which may not be sufficient for in-depth long-term analysis and trend identification. This limitation can hinder the ability to make strategic decisions based on historical performance data.

Another significant limitation of Google Search Console is its lack of features related to backlink analysis and backlink building strategies. Backlinks, or inbound links from other websites to your site, are a fundamental component of SEO and can have a profound impact on a website's domain ranking and authority. However, Google Search Console does not provide tools or insights related to backlinks.

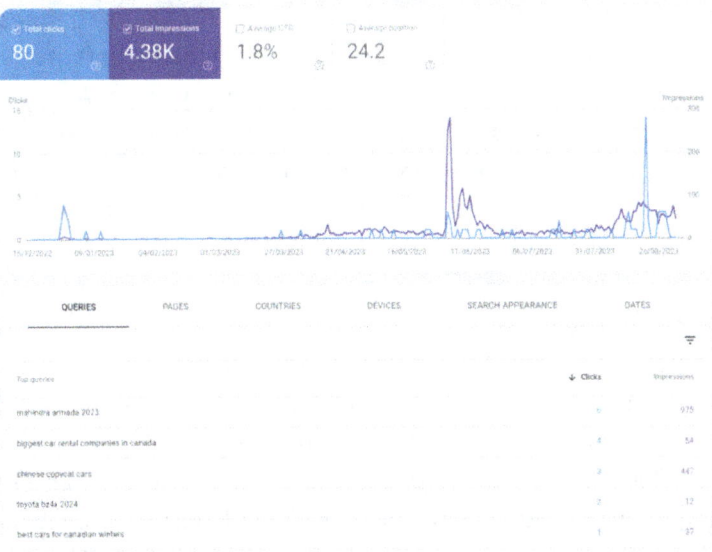

In this context (refer to image), Google Search Console serves as a valuable tool concentrating on informing users about the search queries that lead to their content being displayed in Google's search results. **However, one limitation of Search Console is its inability to provide specific details about the position or ranking at which the content appears in these search results.** This can leave webmasters with a gap in their understanding of their content's visibility and competitiveness in the search landscape.

GSC also provides data for indexed and non-indexed pages along with the feature of requesting for an index. GSC serves as a very powerful tool for assessing the strength of your website.

Further, Google Analytics offers a more comprehensive set of insights to complement the data provided by Search Console. Beyond just search queries, Analytics dives deep into a multitude of critical metrics. For instance, it sheds light on the geographical locations from which a website garners the most traffic, allowing website owners to tailor their content and marketing efforts accordingly. Additionally, Google Analytics provides valuable data on user behavior within web pages, such as how long visitors stay on a site, which pages they visit, and what actions they take, providing a deeper understanding of audience engagement.

Google Analytics includes features such as tracking traffic sources, demographic and interest information about website visitors, conversion tracking, and bounce rate analysis. It allows you to set up and monitor conversion goals, crucial for assessing the effectiveness of a website's objectives. Analytics also offers insights into page performance, including load times, enabling optimization efforts to enhance user experience. Event tracking allows for monitoring specific user interactions, while e-commerce tracking is invaluable for online businesses, offering data on revenue, transactions, and product performance.

Custom reports and dashboards within Google Analytics empower users to tailor their data analysis to match their unique business goals and key performance indicators (KPIs). Additionally, audience segmentation tools enable the creation of targeted content and marketing campaigns by categorizing users based on various criteria.

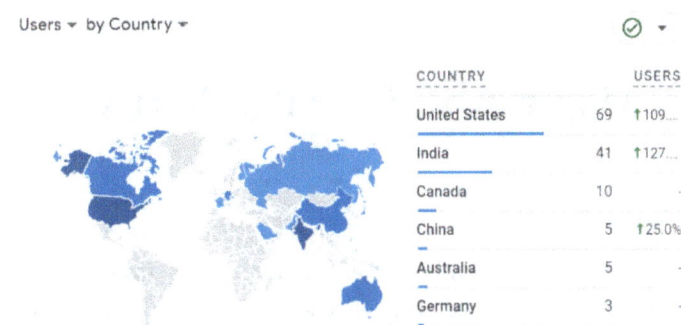

In this image, you can observe that Google Analytics is displaying a crucial key performance indicator, which is the geographical distribution of the user base. However, it lacks the metrics to reveal the specific keywords and their rankings in different countries.

The central point emphasized in this chapter is that while Google Search Console serves as a valuable resource for gaining insights into the internal performance of your website, especially when used alongside its complementary tool, Google Analytics, it falls short in providing an external assessment of your website's relative position on search engine pages.

8

Using Ahrefs and SEMrush

In the preceding chapter, we discussed the importance of Google Search Console and Google Analytics as indispensable tools for monitoring and gaining insights into our websites' internal performance. Now, in this chapter, our focus will shift towards exploring the assessment of external website performance. Here, we will examine the pivotal role played by tools like SEMrush, Ahrefs, or their equivalents in evaluating the broader external aspects of our websites.

Using only Google Search Console and Google Analytics is like participating in a race with blinders on. While you can monitor your own performance and speed, you remain oblivious to what other racecar drivers are doing. You can't see their top speeds or learn from their techniques to improve your driving skills and make your car perform better.

Using Ahrefs and SEMrush in addition to Google Search Console and Google Analytics is like removing those blinders and gaining a broader perspective in the race. It's like having access to a high-tech pit crew that not only tells you how fast your car is going but also provides you with real-time data on what other racecar drivers are doing.

With these tools, you can see the top speeds of your competitors, analyze their driving techniques, and identify the strategies that make them successful. It's like having a dashboard that displays the entire race track, showing you the twists, turns, and shortcuts you can take to improve your own performance. Ahrefs and SEMrush act as your race analysts, helping you make informed decisions about when to accelerate, when to brake, and when to overtake. They provide insights into your competitors' strategies, backlink profiles, and keyword rankings, allowing you to fine-tune your own approach and stay ahead in the race for online visibility and success.

Even the free versions of these tools offer valuable assistance, acting as a ticket to enter the race. They provide essential insights and data that can help you understand the basics of your website's performance and the competitive landscape. It's like getting a taste of the race without committing to the full course. With the free versions, you can start tracking your website's keywords, backlinks, and overall health. It's like having a basic training session before hitting the track. This initial information can guide your efforts and help you make some improvements.

As you gain experience and see the benefits of using these tools, you can consider upgrading to the paid versions. Starting with the free versions is like taking your first step onto the racetrack. It's a smart way to begin your journey towards optimizing your website's performance and achieving better results online.

When SEMrush or Ahrefs seamlessly integrate with Google Search Console, it's like having a complete dashboard for both internal and external analytics. It's as if you're equipped with a high-tech racing control panel that not only displays your car's speed but also tracks the live map of the race circuit, ensuring you have full control over your race.

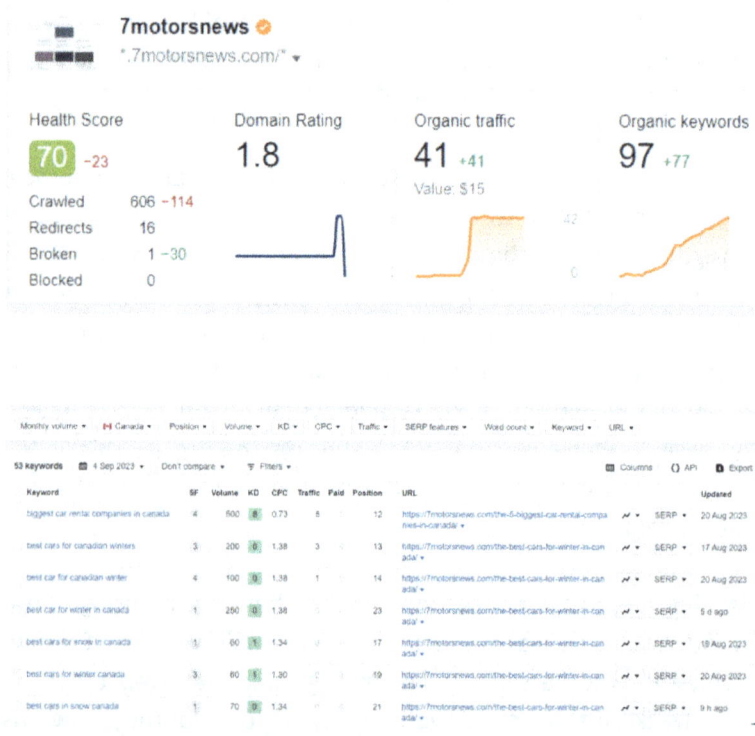

While Ahrefs and SEMrush utilize data from your Google Analytics, they excel in providing a seamless and convenient way to monitor Search Engine Result Pages (SERPs) for keywords that people are searching for on Google in various countries.

9

Improving On Page SEO

As we've discussed in the previous chapters about On-page SEO, we've learned how to use helpful tools like Yoast, Rank Math, or AIOSEO to make our content better. We've also explored tools like Google Bard and Chat GPT to help us organize our content on a webpage or blog. However, there's still much more to discover when it comes to improving On-page SEO, especially when it involves creating a user-friendly webpage with a great user experience and an attractive design.

In this chapter, we'll get deeper into these aspects to make our web content even more effective and appealing to both users and search engines.

While achieving great content readability through tools like Yoast is essential, it's equally crucial to prioritize the overall user experience (UX) of your website. This is vital to minimize the bounce rate, as Google's search engine algorithm penalizes websites with high bounce rates.

When visitors to your website find themselves confused about what actions to take, struggle with navigation, or encounter readability issues with elements like button text or color choices that make buttons difficult to read, it can have a detrimental impact on your website's SEO. It's essential to recognize that UX indirectly affects SEO, and its influence can be significant.

A smooth and user-friendly experience not only keeps visitors engaged but also encourages them to explore your content further, reducing bounce rates and sending positive signals to search engines.

Achieving success in the digital landscape is a delicate balancing act. It's not just about pleasing Google's search engine algorithms; you also need to ensure that your website makes its users happy. This dual challenge can be quite demanding.

To meet this challenge, organizations often assemble a team with diverse skill sets or hire an external agency. UX designers play a pivotal role in crafting a user-friendly website flow, ensuring that visitors can navigate with ease and satisfaction. On the other hand, copywriters focus on making the content SEO-friendly, weaving in relevant keywords and optimizing the text for search engine visibility.

However, the real magic happens when these on-page improvements, driven by UX designers and copywriters, are seamlessly integrated into the broader SEO strategy. This is where growth hackers come into play. They take the user-centric and SEO-friendly improvements and blend them with off-page SEO and technical SEO strategies. This holistic approach ensures that your website not only ranks well in search results but also offers a top-notch user experience, keeping both Google and your audience satisfied.

This multidisciplinary collaboration is the key to mastering the intricate dance of satisfying both search engine algorithms and human users, making it a challenging yet rewarding endeavor in the world of online presence and SEO optimization.

In this context, you'll notice that the button on the right offers improved readability, which means visitors are likely to experience less cognitive strain when deciding to explore your website. While this may not adversely affect the algorithms of search engines, it can leave a negative impression on your webpage's visitors. This negative impression can translate into a higher bounce rate, where visitors quickly leave your site after arriving, and this, in turn, has a direct impact on your website's SEO performance. Therefore, it's essential to ensure that all user interface elements and the overall user flow are designed in a way that provides a positive user experience for anyone visiting your website, ultimately contributing to improved SEO results.

In addition to UX design, it's crucial to prioritize mobile optimization for your website. Ensuring an optimized user experience (UX) on mobile devices involves creating a user-friendly flow on the page. This includes making sure that fonts are easily readable, buttons are responsive, and other elements are mobile-friendly. Google places preference on displaying websites that excel in mobile optimization, aligning with its mobile-first approach.

Also make sure that Header tags are used properly. Header

tags are HTML elements (H1, H2, H3, etc.) used to define headings and subheadings within a web page's content. They not only help organize the content hierarchically but also provide visual cues to readers and search engines about the page's structure and the importance of each section. Ideally, a web page should have only one H1 header tag. The H1 tag is typically used for the main page title or heading, providing a clear and concise summary of the page's topic or subject. Having a single H1 tag helps search engines understand the primary focus of the page and its relevance to search queries. It also aids users in quickly grasping the main idea of the content.

Heading tags, including H2, H3, and beyond, are HTML elements used to structure content on a webpage. H2 tags serve as section headings within the content, breaking it into distinct topics. H3 tags further divide sections into subtopics, providing clarity and organization. Tags like H4-H6 offer additional levels of hierarchy for complex content. Properly using these heading tags enhances content readability, aids navigation, and improves SEO by signaling content hierarchy to search engines.

Adding alt text to images is a vital practice for both web accessibility and search engine optimization (SEO). Alt text, or alternative text, serves as a textual description of an image, ensuring that users with visual impairments can understand the content. When crafting alt text, it's crucial to strike a balance between conciseness and descriptiveness, providing a brief but meaningful summary of the image's purpose. Avoid redundancy by not duplicating surrounding text, and if an image is purely decorative, use empty alt text. For images with text, include that text in the alt description, and for informative images like charts or graphs, provide alt text that conveys the data or message. Remember to test your alt text with screen readers to ensure it enhances accessibility, making your website inclusive for all users while also contributing to SEO efforts by providing context to search engines.

In alt text, it's essential to avoid certain practices to ensure that it serves its intended purpose effectively. Firstly, steer clear of keyword stuffing, where you overload alt text with keywords in an attempt to manipulate SEO rankings. Alt text should provide natural and relevant descriptions of images. Additionally, avoid redundancy by refraining from duplicating text already present on the webpage or within image captions. Alt text should complement and enhance the content.

Another aspect to avoid is crafting excessively long or complex alt text, as it can be overwhelming for users relying on screen readers. Similarly, generic or vague descriptions should be avoided; alt text should convey the image's purpose or content clearly and concisely. **Malpractice in alt images, such as keyword stuffing, inaccuracies, empty alt text, or disregarding accessibility standards, can have a detrimental effect on your website's SEO.** Properly formatted and descriptive alt text not only enhances accessibility but also provides valuable context to search engines, contributing to improved search engine rankings and a better overall user experience.

10

Improving Technical SEO

Technical SEO refers to the process of optimizing the technical aspects of your website to improve its search engine visibility and performance. This facet of SEO focuses on ensuring that search engine crawlers can easily access, index, and understand your website's content. Here are key elements and practices associated with technical SEO:

Website Speed

Ensure your website loads quickly on both desktop and mobile devices. Slow-loading pages can lead to higher bounce rates and negatively impact SEO. Tools like Google Page Speed Insights can help identify areas for improvement.

Here are the following aspects that needs to be improved to improve a website's loading speed:

Image Optimization:
Compression: Reduce image file sizes without significantly compromising quality using image compression tools.

Lazy Loading: Load images only when they come into the user's viewport, saving bandwidth and reducing initial page load time.

Responsive Images: Serve appropriately sized images based on the user's device and screen resolution.

Minimize HTTP Requests:

Combine Files: Minimize the number of external CSS and JavaScript files by combining and minifying them.

Use CSS Sprites: Combine multiple small images into a single sprite image to reduce HTTP requests.
Use Icon Fonts: Replace multiple small images with icon fonts to reduce requests.

Caching:

Implement browser caching to store static assets locally on a user's device, reducing the need to re-download them on subsequent visits.

Content Delivery Network (CDN):

Use a CDN to distribute website content to servers geographically closer to the user, reducing latency and improving load times.

Eliminate Render-Blocking Resources:

Minimize or defer the loading of CSS and JavaScript resources that block the rendering of the page.

Crawlability and Indexability

Crawlability and indexability are two fundamental concepts in search engine optimization (SEO) that directly impact how search engines discover and rank your website's content. Understanding these concepts and optimizing your website accordingly is crucial for achieving better visibility in search engine results pages (SERPs).

Crawlability:

Crawlability refers to a search engine's ability to navigate and explore the content of your website. When a search engine's crawler (also known as a spider or bot) visits your site, it follows links to access various pages and resources. If your site is not crawlable, important pages and content may remain undiscovered, negatively affecting your search engine rankings.

Effects of Poor Crawlability:

Pages Not Indexed: If a search engine cannot crawl your website effectively, it may not index all your pages, meaning they won't appear in search results.
Missed SEO Opportunities: Poor crawlability can lead to missed opportunities to rank for relevant keywords and topics.

Optimizing Crawlability:

Robots.txt: Use a robots.txt file to instruct search engine crawlers on which parts of your website should be crawled and which should not.

XML Sitemaps: Create XML sitemaps to provide search engines with a list of your website's pages, helping them discover and crawl content efficiently.

Clean URL Structure: Use clean, user-friendly URLs that are easy for both search engines and users to understand.

Internal Linking: Implement a strong internal linking structure to help search engines discover and navigate through your site's pages.

Indexability:

Indexability is a critical aspect of search engine optimization (SEO) that directly influences a website's visibility and performance in search engine results. It refers to the search engine's decision to include or exclude a web page from its index, which is the vast database of web pages that search engines use to provide search results to users. Even if a page is successfully crawled by search engine bots, it may not be indexed if it's considered low-quality or irrelevant to search queries.

Here's how indexability affects websites:

Visibility in Search Results: Indexability determines whether a web page has the opportunity to appear in search engine results pages (SERPs). Indexed pages have a chance to rank for relevant keywords and phrases, increasing their visibility to potential visitors.

Traffic and User Engagement: Indexed pages are more likely to receive organic traffic from search engines. When a page is excluded from the index, it misses out on the opportunity to attract users searching for related information, products, or services.

SEO Performance: Pages that are indexed contribute to the overall SEO performance of a website. They help build domain authority and improve the website's chances of ranking well in search results.

Content Relevance: Indexability is closely tied to content quality and relevance. Search engines assess the content on a page to determine whether it provides value to users. Low-quality, spammy, or irrelevant content is less likely to be indexed.

Crawling Efficiency: Search engines aim to allocate their resources efficiently. When they encounter low-quality or duplicate content that shouldn't be indexed, they waste time and resources crawling and processing it. This can slow down the indexing of more valuable content.

User Experience: Indexed pages typically offer valuable information or resources to users. When search engines exclude low-quality or irrelevant pages, they contribute to a better overall user experience by presenting users with more meaningful search results.

Optimizing for Indexability:

To ensure that your web pages are indexed and contribute positively to your website's SEO, consider the following optimization strategies:

Create High-Quality Content: Produce valuable, unique, and well-researched content that addresses the needs and interests of your target audience.

Optimize Meta Tags: Craft compelling title tags and meta descriptions that accurately represent the content of each page and entice users to click through from search results.

Mobile Optimization: Ensure that your website is mobile-friendly, as mobile usability is a key factor in search engine indexability.

Fix Duplicate Content: Address duplicate content issues by using canonical tags to specify the preferred version of a page and avoiding duplicate meta tags and descriptions.

Maintain a Clean Site Structure: Organize your website's structure and navigation to make it easy for search engine crawlers to access and understand your content.
Monitor Indexation: Regularly check your website's indexation status using tools like Google Search Console and address any indexability issues promptly.

Improve Website Structure

Improving your website structure is essential for enhancing user experience, search engine optimization (SEO), and overall website performance. A well-structured website not only helps visitors navigate seamlessly but also makes it easier for search engines to understand and rank your content. Here are key steps to improve your website's structure:

Define Clear Goals and Objectives: Before making structural changes, establish clear goals for your website. Understand what you want to achieve, whether it's increasing sales, providing information, or building a community. Your structure should align with these objectives.

Create a Logical Hierarchy: Organize your website's content into a clear and logical hierarchy. Think of it as a tree structure, with a homepage at the top and categories and subcategories branching out beneath it.

User-Centered Navigation: Design your navigation menus with the user in mind. Use descriptive labels that convey the content's purpose, and keep menus simple and easy to understand. Consider using drop-down menus or mega-menus for complex sites.

Breadcrumb Navigation: Breadcrumbs are a visual aid that shows users their current location on your site and helps them backtrack if needed. They also provide contextual information to search engines.

Content Silos: Organize your content into themed "silos" or groups. This makes it easier for both users and search engines to find and navigate related content.

301 Redirects: If you make structural changes or update URLs, use 301 redirects to ensure that old URLs redirect to the new ones. This preserves SEO value and prevents broken links.

Consistent Design and Branding: Maintain a consistent design and branding throughout your website. Consistency helps build trust and recognition among your audience.

Schema Markup: Implement schema markup (structured data) to provide search engines with additional context about your content, helping them display rich snippets in search results.

User Testing: Conduct user testing to gather feedback on your website's structure and navigation. This can help you identify and address usability issues.

HTTPS and Security

HTTPS and Security for Hosting Providers (Hostinger, HostGator, Bluehost, Azure, and AWS etc):

Ensuring the security of your website is a paramount concern, regardless of the hosting provider or platform you choose. Here's how you can achieve HTTPS security on popular hosting providers like Hostinger, HostGator, and Bluehost, as well as on robust platforms like Azure and AWS:

1. Hostinger, HostGator, and Bluehost

If you're hosting your website with providers like Hostinger, HostGator, or Bluehost, achieving HTTPS security is relatively straightforward:

a. Obtain an SSL/TLS Certificate: These hosting providers typically offer SSL/TLS certificate options that you can purchase or include for free in some hosting plans. Alternatively, you can obtain a certificate from a reputable Certificate Authority (CA).

b. Install and Configure the Certificate: Follow the hosting provider's documentation to install and configure the SSL/TLS certificate on your website. This process is often simplified through the hosting control panel.

c. Update Website Links and Resources: Ensure that all internal links and resources (such as images, scripts, and stylesheets) on your website use HTTPS instead of HTTP. This step prevents mixed content issues and browser warnings.

d. Update .htaccess File (for Apache Servers): If you're using an Apache server, update your .htaccess file to enforce HTTPS. You can add code that redirects HTTP requests to HTTPS.

e. Update Search Engine Settings: Notify search engines of your HTTPS migration by updating your sitemap and robots.txt file. Additionally, consider setting up 301 redirects from HTTP to HTTPS URLs.

2. Robust Platforms and Hard-Coded Websites

If your website is hard-coded or hosted on a more robust platform, such as Microsoft Azure (Azure) or Amazon Web Services (AWS), achieving HTTPS security is equally important:

a. Obtain an SSL/TLS Certificate: You can obtain SSL/TLS certificates from trusted CAs, even if your website is hosted on Azure or AWS. The process may involve some manual configuration.

b. Install and Configure the Certificate: Follow the documentation provided by Azure or AWS to install and configure the SSL/TLS certificate on your server or load balancer.

c. Update Website Code: If your website is hard-coded, you'll need to update the code to ensure that all resource references use HTTPS. This includes links to stylesheets, scripts, and external resources.

d. Enforce HTTPS: Configure your web server or application to enforce HTTPS connections. This may involve modifying server settings, security groups, or load balancer rules.

Mobile Optimization

Mobile optimization is crucial in today's digital landscape, as more users access websites from mobile devices. Achieving a well-optimized mobile experience involves understanding concepts like the waterfall model and adaptive design.

Here's an overview of these concepts and how to achieve mobile optimization for both hard-coded websites and those built using website builders like WordPress:

1. Waterfall Model: The waterfall model represents a linear approach to web page loading. In this model, assets (e.g., HTML, CSS, JavaScript, images) are loaded one after the other, which can lead to slower page load times on mobile devices. To optimize mobile performance using the waterfall model:

a. Minimize Render-Blocking Resources: Identify and minimize resources that block the rendering of the page, such as external CSS and JavaScript. Use asynchronous or deferred loading to improve loading speed.

b. Optimize Images: Compress images, use modern formats like WebP, and implement lazy loading to reduce image-related performance issues.

2. Adaptive Design: Adaptive design involves creating different versions of a website for various device types, such as mobile phones, tablets, and desktops. Each version is tailored to the specific screen size and capabilities of the device. To achieve adaptive design:

a. Media Queries: Use CSS media queries to apply different styles and layouts based on the screen width. This allows for a responsive design that adapts to various devices.

b. Device Detection: Implement server-side device detection to serve different HTML templates or layouts based on the user's device.

Mobile Optimization in WordPress Websites

For websites built with WordPress, you can achieve mobile optimization by:

Choose a Mobile-Friendly Theme: Select a responsive

WordPress theme that adapts to different screen sizes. Many modern themes are mobile-responsive by default.

Use Mobile Optimization Plugins:
WP Super Cache: Caches your website to improve page load times.
WPtouch: Adds a mobile-friendly theme for better mobile user experience.
Smush: Compresses and optimizes images to reduce file sizes.
WP Fastest Cache: Provides caching and optimization features to improve site speed.
Test on Mobile Devices: Regularly test your WordPress website on various mobile devices to ensure it looks and functions correctly.

Mobile Optimization in Hard-Coded Websites

For hard-coded websites, you can achieve mobile optimization by:

Responsive Design: Implement responsive web design principles using CSS media queries to adapt your site's layout and content based on screen size.

Optimize Images: Compress and resize images for smaller screens, and use responsive image techniques like the <picture> element or the srcset attribute to serve appropriately sized images.

Mobile-Friendly Navigation: Ensure that navigation menus and interactive elements are touch-friendly and easy to use on mobile devices.

Minimizing Server Response Times

Minimizing server response times is a critical aspect of optimizing website performance and directly affects the time it takes for a web page to load. Even small improvements in server response times can lead to better user experiences and SEO progress.

Here's how it can impact your website and the factors to consider:

Impact on Website Response Time:

Server response time, often referred to as Time to First Byte (TTFB), measures the time it takes for a user's browser to receive the first byte of data from the web server after making a request. It plays a crucial role in determining the overall page load time, which directly affects user satisfaction and SEO rankings. Faster server response times result in quicker page rendering, providing a better user experience. **Users are more likely to engage with and stay on a website that loads quickly**. **Google and other search engines use page load times as a ranking factor. Websites with faster server response times are more likely to rank higher in search engine results pages (SERPs), contributing to SEO progress.**

Factors Affecting Server Response Time:

a. Server Configuration: Server configuration is vital for ensuring your website can effectively manage incoming traffic and avoid crashes or slowdowns. To achieve this, you must allocate adequate CPU, RAM, and storage resources to your server and be prepared to scale up when traffic spikes occur.

Implementing load balancing helps evenly distribute traffic among multiple servers, preventing overloads on any single server and ensuring performance and redundancy. Leveraging a Content Delivery Network (CDN) is another key strategy, reducing latency and enhancing content delivery for users across the globe. Additionally, server-side caching mechanisms like Varnish and Redis can optimize performance by storing frequently accessed data and lightening the server's load. Proper server configuration and maintenance are critical for providing a seamless user experience, even during periods of high traffic.

b. Image Optimization: Image optimization is pivotal for website performance, influencing loading times and user satisfaction. Large image files can hinder site speed, diminishing the user experience. To trim file sizes, manually adjust image dimensions, pick suitable formats, and strip unnecessary metadata before uploading. In WordPress, plugins such as Imagify or ShortPixel automate WebP conversion. For non-WordPress websites, like custom-coded ones, automation can be achieved by incorporating WebP conversion libraries into your codebase. Additionally, online tools like TinyPNG, Squoosh, or ezgif.com can optimize and convert images. Regularly auditing and substituting older, uncompressed images is essential for continual performance enhancement.

c. Caching: Caching is a process that stores previously generated web content, such as web pages or data, to reduce the time and resources required to serve user requests. When a user visits a site, cached content can be delivered quickly, bypassing the need to regenerate it from scratch, thus significantly reducing server response times. This efficient reuse of data improves website performance and user experience, making caching a vital tool for optimizing server response times. Caching, particularly when combined with cookies, is a technique that stores and retrieves previously generated web content or user data, reducing server response times. Cookies play a role by storing user-specific information or preferences, allowing cached content to be personalized for each user. This efficient reuse of data, tailored to individual users, enhances website performance and user experience, making caching with cookies a powerful tool for optimizing server response times and delivering a more customized online experience.

d. Database Optimization: Database optimization is important for both hard-coded websites and those built on content management systems (CMS) like WordPress.

Here's why:

1. Hard-Coded Websites: In hard-coded websites, where the code is manually written, efficient database design and query optimization are essential. This is because developers have full control over the database schema and queries. If the database is not well-structured or queries are poorly optimized, it can lead to slow page load times and reduced performance.

2. WordPress or Similar CMS: Content management systems like WordPress rely heavily on databases to store and retrieve content, user data, and settings. While these systems offer user-friendly interfaces for website management, they can generate complex database queries. As a result, database optimization remains crucial.

Key points for optimization include:

a. Plugin and Theme Efficiency: Poorly coded plugins and themes can generate inefficient database queries. It's essential to choose reputable plugins and themes and regularly update them to maintain performance.

b. Database Cleanup: WordPress stores revisions, spam comments, and other unnecessary data in the database. Regularly cleaning up this data can improve database performance.

c. Caching: Implementing a caching solution can reduce the number of database queries by serving cached content to visitors, especially for static or semi-static pages.

d. Query Optimization: Analyzing and optimizing frequently executed database queries within plugins, themes, or custom code can significantly improve performance.

e. Database Indexing: Properly index tables to speed up data retrieval.

f. Database Management Tools: WordPress provides database management plugins that can help optimize and repair the database tables.

11

Improving Off-Page SEO

Non-technical SEO encompasses a broader spectrum of SEO efforts beyond the individual page level. It includes on-page SEO but also extends to various other SEO strategies that aren't directly related to a webpage's content or structure. This aspect of SEO is known as Off-Page SEO. We have already discussed about it in earlier chapter. In this chapter we will explore various strategies and techniques to improve your website's visibility and rankings in search results.

Social Media Marketing and SEO: Social media marketing plays a vital role in enhancing your website's visibility and overall SEO strategy. It contributes to achieving your desired outcomes, whether it's increasing readership, selling a course, or promoting products.

Here's why social media marketing is crucial for SEO success:

Boosts Visibility and Traffic: Sharing your website content on social media platforms exposes it to a broader audience. When your content gets shared and engages users on social media, it can lead to increased website traffic, which is a positive signal for search engines.

Builds Backlinks: High-quality content shared on social media has the potential to attract backlinks from other websites and blogs. These backlinks improve your website's authority and search engine rankings, a core component of SEO.

Enhances Content Distribution: Social media platforms serve as powerful distribution channels for your content. By strategically promoting your articles, courses, or products, you can reach a wider audience and encourage sharing, thus expanding your online reach.

Content Discovery: Social media platforms facilitate content discovery. When users encounter your content through their social feeds, they may explore your website further, leading to more page views, longer sessions, and improved SEO metrics.

Audience Engagement: Building a loyal follower base through social media allows you to engage with your audience directly. Engaged followers are more likely to visit your website, consume your content, and convert into customers or subscribers.

User-Generated Content: Encouraging user-generated content on social media, such as reviews, testimonials, or user-generated posts, can provide valuable social proof and credibility, further enhancing your website's reputation.

Backlinks from reputable and authoritative websites act as endorsements for your content. When high-quality sites link to yours, it boosts your credibility and trustworthiness in the eyes of search engines and users. They can drive direct referral traffic to your site. When users click on a link from another site to yours, it can result in more visitors who are likely interested in your content or products.

Backlinks are a major factor in calculating a website's domain authority, a metric that reflects a site's overall trustworthiness and influence. High domain authority is often correlated with better search rankings.

Methods to Build Backlinks:

Guest Blogging: Guest blogging on high domain authority websites presents several challenges. Firstly, these sites attract a significant volume of guest post submissions, intensifying competition for publication slots. To succeed, you must offer unique and valuable content ideas that resonate with the site's audience and niche. Secondly, maintaining top-tier content quality is imperative, as these platforms have stringent editorial standards. Any compromise in research, writing, or grammar can lead to rejection. Thirdly, adhering to the site's specific guidelines and formatting requirements is crucial, as even minor deviations can result in your submission being declined. Lastly, ensuring the relevance of your content to both the host site and its readers is essential for achieving success in guest blogging on high DA websites. **A significant consideration when guest blogging on high domain authority websites is the effective use of HARO (Help a Reporter Out).** HARO is a platform that connects journalists and writers with subject matter experts. While it can be a valuable tool for securing guest post opportunities and media mentions, it comes with its own challenges. Firstly, the competition on HARO can be fierce, with countless experts vying for the same media placements. Secondly, it requires a timely response as journalists often have tight deadlines. Being consistently responsive and providing valuable insights is essential.

Influencer Reach out: Influencer outreach is a popular marketing strategy that entails engaging with individuals who wield significant influence within specific niches or industries. Leveraging their reach and credibility can be highly effective for promoting products, services, or content to a wider audience. However, this approach is not without its challenges. One of the foremost difficulties is identifying the right influencers whose followers align with your target demographic, necessitating extensive research and vetting. **Competition is fierce, as influencers receive numerous collaboration requests, making it crucial to craft compelling proposals. Cost is another factor to contend with, as many influencers require compensation.** Additionally, maintaining authenticity in partnerships and ensuring that the influencer's content aligns with your brand values can be complex. Measurement and ROI assessment can also pose challenges. Despite these hurdles, when and how to reach out to influencers depends on your campaign goals, but advance planning is generally advisable.

What to Avoid

While building backlinks, avoid these unethical or risky practices:

Buying Links: Purchasing links is against search engine guidelines and can lead to penalties.
Link Farms: Avoid being part of link farms or excessive reciprocal linking schemes, as they are seen as spammy.

Low-Quality Directories: Submitting your site to low-quality or irrelevant directories can harm your SEO.

Keyword-Stuffed Anchor Text: Using keyword-rich anchor text excessively in backlinks can appear manipulative and lead to penalties.

Negative SEO and Bad Backlinks: Negative SEO involves attempts by competitors or malicious actors to harm your website's rankings or reputation. Bad backlinks from spammy or low-quality sources can be a common tactic in negative SEO campaigns. Regularly monitoring your backlink profile and disavowing toxic links can help mitigate the impact of negative SEO. Backlinks play a crucial role in building domain authority. A website with a higher number of quality backlinks from diverse sources is likely to have higher domain authority. This, in turn, can positively influence search rankings, trustworthiness, and overall online authority.

12

Prepare yourself for AI-Age SEO

Artificial Intelligence (AI) is poised to bring significant changes to the landscape of search engine optimization (SEO). One of the prominent shifts is related to informational keywords.

Let's get into depth of what we learned in the second chapter:

AI-Powered Text Models: AI text models like ChatGPT and Google Bard have become increasingly sophisticated in understanding and responding to natural language queries. This evolution allows them to act as virtual consultants, providing in-depth and contextually relevant information, thereby reducing the need for users to visit multiple websites for answers. AI-driven answer models, like ChatGpt are revolutionizing the way we access and make sense of information on the internet. These models possess immense processing power, capable of handling the vast permutations and combinations of data available online. They tirelessly scour an infinite pool of information sources, extracting and presenting the most relevant content in a matter of seconds.

But their capabilities don't stop there. AI models are quick learners. With each interaction, they gain insights into your preferences, needs, and context, enabling them to continually refine their responses. This personalization is akin to having a knowledgeable assistant who understands you better with every interaction.

It's essential to reflect on how far we've come since the early days of the internet when simply accessing information with a single click felt empowering. However, the landscape is evolving. While websites initially thrived on providing access to information, AI-driven models are now transforming how we engage with this data. **The trend of traditional web browsing and the business models built around it might not sustain in the same way as AI continues to reshape our digital experiences.** The future promises an era where information is not just accessible but deeply personalized and readily available.

Content Discovery and Presentation: AI algorithms, including those used by search engines, are improving at content discovery and presentation. They can surface highly relevant content from various sources, such as articles, videos, and audio, making it more accessible to users. **In this changing landscape, the game of ranking on informational keywords is evolving into a high-stakes competition.** Simply providing information may no longer be enough. The richness and value of the content delivered become paramount. AI can offer quick answers, but content creators have an opportunity to provide deeper insights, context, and a human touch that AI often lacks. This positions content creators and marketers to focus on crafting content that goes beyond surface-level information, catering to an audience that seeks more comprehensive, thoughtful, and engaging content. However, it's worth noting that this audience, craving in-depth insights, may be a niche within the larger online population.

YouTube and Visual Content: YouTube, as a platform for audio-visual content, has gained immense popularity. It offers engaging content in a format that often surpasses traditional text-based information in terms of user appeal. Creators have shifted from websites to YouTube, bringing SEO practices tailored for video content. As a result, YouTube has its own set of algorithms and practices for content visibility and discoverability. AI is making it increasingly easier to produce video content. Neural text-to-speech (TTS) technologies, coupled with AI-driven video editing tools, have streamlined the video creation process. These advancements enable content creators to transform text-based scripts into engaging video presentations with minimal effort. AI-powered TTS systems can generate natural-sounding voiceovers, while basic video editing AI tools can enhance visual elements, transitions, and effects, making video content production more accessible and efficient. This trend further underscores the shift towards visual content as an integral part of modern digital communication.

Navigational keywords are relatively safe in the context of SEO because they typically indicate that users are looking for specific websites or webpages. These keywords are often brand or domain-specific and are used when users want to directly access a particular website or web resource. For example, someone searching for "Facebook login" or "Apple website" is likely trying to navigate directly to these specific sites.

Here's why navigational keywords are safe:

Clear User Intent: Navigational keywords have a clear user intent—to find a specific website or webpage. Search engines understand this intent and aim to provide the most relevant and direct result, which is often the homepage of the requested website.

Low Competition: Since navigational keywords are usually tied to a specific brand or website, there is typically little competition from other websites. As a result, ranking for these keywords is often straightforward, especially if you own or manage the website in question.

Branded Queries: Many navigational keywords are branded queries, which means they include the name of a specific brand or company. When users search for a brand directly, they are often already familiar with it and have a strong intent to visit that brand's website.

Low SEO Risk: There is minimal risk of SEO challenges or penalties associated with optimizing for navigational keywords. These keywords are generally straightforward and don't involve the complexities or ambiguities of informational or transactional queries.

Commercial keywords, often associated with transactional intent, are generally considered safe in the realm of SEO for several reasons:

Clear Purchase Intent: Commercial keywords reflect users' intent to make a purchase or engage in a transaction. They are specific and often indicate that users are ready to convert, making them valuable for businesses.

Lower Competition: Commercial keywords often have less competition compared to informational keywords, as they are typically more niche-specific. This can make it easier for businesses to rank for these keywords within their industry.

Revenue Generation: Ranking for commercial keywords can directly contribute to revenue generation, making them a priority for businesses looking to boost sales and conversions.

we are officially in the AI age, and AI is becoming increasingly pervasive in digital platforms and services. Just as electricity revolutionized various industries by enabling the development of electronic devices, AI is transforming how websites and digital products operate and interact with users.

AI-driven websites like ChatGPT, Midjourney, and others are examples of the growing trend in AI-powered online services. These websites offer advanced capabilities, such as natural language understanding, personalized recommendations, and interactive experiences that were not possible with traditional websites.

The choice of keywords is not one-size-fits-all; it varies based on the intent behind the content. Here's a breakdown:

1. Informational Keywords: When targeting informational keywords, the objective is to provide the most comprehensive and detailed content on a specific topic. AI can assist in understanding the nuances of user intent and what constitutes a comprehensive answer. Content creators should aim to be the best source of information on the chosen topic, covering it comprehensively and addressing various facets of the subject.

2. Navigational Keywords: Navigational keywords are often associated with specific actions, such as finding an affiliate page or accessing a login page. In these cases, the emphasis may be less on detailed content and more on creating a user-friendly, efficient pathway to the desired action. While AI can help optimize navigation and user experience, simplicity and clarity in design and content presentation are key.

3. Commercial Keywords: Commercial keywords indicate an intent to make a purchase or engage in a transaction. When targeting these keywords, content creators can have a level of confidence, as these keywords often signal a readiness to convert. However, competition may be high, so optimizing for conversion and providing a seamless user experience are essential. AI can assist in personalizing content and offers to enhance the chances of conversion.

In this AI-driven era of SEO, success hinges on understanding user intent and tailoring content accordingly. By aligning keyword strategies with the specific intent behind searches, content creators can harness the power of AI to enhance on-page SEO, deliver valuable content, and ultimately drive meaningful results in the ever-evolving digital landscape.

Use conversational keywords: When creating content, use keywords and phrases that people are likely to use when speaking, rather than typing. For example, instead of "best Italian restaurants in New York City," you could use "where to find good Italian food in NYC."

Create long-form content: People are more likely to ask conversational questions about complex topics. By creating long-form content that answers these questions in detail, you can improve your chances of ranking for conversational searches. You can use text to voice plug-in on your website for enhancing UX.

Use natural language: When writing your content, use natural language and avoid jargon. This will make it easier for search engines to understand the meaning of your content and rank it higher for conversational searches.

Optimize your website for voice search: Voice search is becoming increasingly popular, so it's important to optimize your website for this type of search. This includes using conversational keywords and phrases, as well as creating content that is easy to understand and navigate.

The probability of Google adapting conversational SEO preferences is high. As more and more people use voice search and other conversational search methods, Google will need to adapt its algorithm to reflect these changes. This means that websites that are optimized for conversational SEO will be more likely to rank high in search results.

Here are some additional things to keep in mind when optimizing your website for conversational SEO:

Focus on user intent: When creating content, focus on what the user is trying to achieve. What are they looking for? What information do they need? By understanding the user's intent, you can create content that is more likely to rank high for conversational searches.

Use schema markup: Schema markup is a way to tell search engines about the structure and meaning of your content. This can help to improve your ranking for conversational searches, as well as other types of searches.

Keep your content up-to-date: Search engines prefer to rank websites with fresh, up-to-date content. Make sure to regularly update your content with new information and insights.

Conversational insights by GSC and GA: AI-powered analytics provide deeper insights into user behavior and preferences. We might expect more refined versions of Google Search Console and Google Analytics that gives more conversational insights to us.

Potential Threat to the concept of SEO

The potential threat to SEO doesn't stem from conventional internet experiences on flat screens, such as those on mobile devices, iPads, or laptops. The more imminent challenge lies in emerging concepts like the metaverse, where the very notion of traditional search engines might eventually become less relevant. However, it's essential to note that the full realization of the metaverse for the masses is still on the horizon, and there are several formidable obstacles to overcome. Hardware limitations, server capacities, and network speeds are among the significant challenges that need to be addressed before the metaverse can become a seamless and practical reality. As a result, SEO is likely to remain a critical part of digital strategies for at least the next decade because traditional search engines will continue to play a vital role in the current digital landscape.

In the age of flat screens, whether on our mobile devices, laptops, or tablets, the significance of SEO remains steadfast. While the landscape of search engine optimization may undergo shifts, such as the evolving challenges of ranking on informational keywords, one thing is clear: SEO is here to stay.

However, as we peer into the future, the emergence of the metaverse promises a transformative impact on how we interact with digital realms. This immersive virtual space has the potential to reshape our online experiences entirely. While it may seem insignificant at that moment, SEO remains too crucial to overlook, at least for the upcoming decade!